June 2024
ISBN-979-8-9855592-5-5

Broken Ever After

Selected Poems

JEFFREY CHARLES
KINARD

To Anika

BROKEN EVER AFTER

BROKEN EVER AFTER

SELECTED POEMS

THE SKY

I remember the forest
I remember the trees
I remember dancing
underneath the leaves
  and the sky

  Oh, the sky
  So high and empty
  clouds the size of mountains
  floating by

  Filling my eyes
  All will be
  until I die

I remember the campsite
I remember the dark
I remember the fire
spilling all of its sparks
  to the sky

  Oh, the sky
  The vortex of the stars
  lifts me from the earth
  like I could fly

  Filling my eyes
  All will be
  until I die

DUST DEVIL

I was born to follow
that which does not lead
I've been chasing dust devils
since I was seventeen

I'm a little dusty
Look-a-bit like the road
Long and straight and open-faced
Getting gray and old

> The endless sky
> The churning winds
> Following the signs
> along a trail of coincidence
> Never going home again

> The rabbit brush
> The red dirt hills
> The dust of the Earth
> belongs wherever it cares to swirl
> Until the end of the world

All these tired crossroads
in all these sun-baked towns
Full of coyote people
if you really look around

Watchers talk their stories
to lizards with no eyes
While I'm here at the crossroads
watching the train go by

The endless sky
The churning winds
Following the signs
along a trail of coincidence
Never going home again

The rabbit brush
The red dirt hills
The dust of the Earth
belongs wherever it cares to swirl
Until the end of the world

A rusty old tin sign
in the faintest breeze
Catch sight of a devil
and I'm on my way due east

I was born to follow
that which does not lead
I've been chasing dust devils
since I was seventeen

NOBODY SHOWED

Nobody showed
for the party you threw
on the evening
of the new year
Nobody knew
all the hours you slaved
over crab cakes
and French canapes

I spied on you
and you didn't know
I was hiding near the base
of the stairs
I didn't know
just how sad it was
to drink champagne
all alone

Pink party dress
A spill but you didn't care
Your hair had fallen and the ice
was gone
You called us to come
brother and I
We came downstairs slow
because you forbade

We watched the countdown
on that old TV
It was the first time I remember
New Year's

H E A R T

If I'm ever gonna be untrue
it will be to me and not to you
Awkward phases that I'm going through
When I'm going through
What I'm going through

Often seem to be these little gaps
'tween what's in my heart and where I'm at
Suddenly I'm neither this nor that
Don't know my heart
Don't know where I'm at

> No matter how lost I am
> I can follow my heart again
> It's the only way for you
> to live and die doing
> what you want to do

Now maybe my heart is always right
The courage to follow takes all my might
When the path leads into darkest night
Facing the old ghosts
stealing my light

Of anything, there is one thing clear
The enemy of my heart is fear
Of course, you know what I'm speaking of
Fear of pain is also
fear of love

> No matter how lost I am
> I can follow my heart again
> It's the only way for you
> to live and die doing
> what you want to do

CAREFREE (FOR CAROLYN)

Upon a hilltop
Under a tree
Nothing but blue sky
My motorcycle
And me...
And me...

Today is the day
I rode away
Unplugged my whole life
Made my escape
I'm free...
I'm free...

      No job, no rent, no bills to pay
      No clocks ticking my time away
      No meters turning through the day
      to slowly drain my cash away
      Insane

I have a small tent
A box of paints
Dirty coveralls
Gas in the tank
And me...
I've got me...

What is my next move?
Just wait and see
I'm doing nothing
and nothing's doing me
I'm free...
I'm free...

I had to go, I had no choice
I could not stay and have no joy
I broke the square, threw it away
Maybe I'll move into a cave
and paint

Upon a hilltop
Under a tree
Nothing but blue sky
My motorcycle
And me...
And me...

What is my next move?
Just wait and see
I'm doing nothing
and nothing's doing me
I'm free...
I'm free...

Somewhere someone's damning me
for all the things I cannot be
But it's just me beneath this tree
Nowhere to go, no one to be
Carefree

JUST GONE

Waking up at dawn the windows steamed
Everything I own
is in this truck with me
Hop outside to piss on the side of the road
Drifting mist in the green mountains
and it's cold cold cold

Just a splash of water to brush my teeth
Shift the load from sleeping mode
rubbing my hands for heat
The engine starts up on the second try
She ain't new, but I'll tell you
she is better than alright

> The road is long
> And I didn't expect to just be gone
> But here I am
> (just gone)
> In my rolling home
> ten thousand miles from where I've been

All these hours behind the wheel to think
But I just like the always moving
blur of everything
The feel of the wheels never turning back
If I get lost maybe I'll find
someplace not on the map

Truck stop shower and a sleep between the rigs
Sometimes the only way
not to get hassled by the pigs
Out to the desert underneath the moon
In the sea of loneliness
'til it turns to solitude

The road is long
And I didn't expect to just be gone
But here I am
(just gone)
Standing all alone
with no idea where I belong

Driven through 46 of the 50 states
After a while I would like
just to look at another face
Pull off into a diner for a rest
Blow my last few bucks on sweet talk
and a breakfast mess

Another day another speed-trap town
Maybe I'll find a bit of work
if I stick around
Trade my time for supplies and a tank of gas
Heading south from here
and I'm never coming back

The road is long
And I didn't expect to just be gone
But here I am
(just gone)
Wandering along
Happy until I'm broken down

REAL AS A GHOST

There's not too much gonna hold me down
I'm as real as a ghost
when the walls come down

Today I'm playing tic tac toe
Tomorrow I'm playing tag
It's olly olly oxen free
when no one gives a damn

By the old gods and the new
and everything else that's inside of you
I will do what I will say
My word is my bond
until my dying day

There's not too much gonna run me 'round
I may not look like much
Ninety percent underground

I'm doing only what I want
Wanting only what I need
You can keep the rest of it
I'll keep it lean and mean

By the old gods and the new
and everything else that's inside of you
I will do what I will say
My word is my bond
upon the boundless way

There's not too much keeps me in this town
I've walked every shadow
that my fear has found

Knowing I know nothing at all
Another folly for the wise
My eyes open like eagle wings
when the northern winds arise

    By the old gods and the new
    and everything else that's inside of you
    I will do what I will say
    My word is my bond
    until my words change

MANHATTAN

New York City
been so good for me
I've walked Manhattan
and Manhattan has walked me
She'll treat you so shitty
before revealing her beauty
Anything less
than great success
she's not intrigued

In California
I lost my heart again
I tried to warn ya
I was damaged and broken
If a man falls in the city
I know no one will hear him
When he moans
he moans alone
It's good for him

I almost died
Alcohol poisoning
I slept outside
in the winter wind
I had nowhere left to go
you were the only place I lived
My frozen bones
I should have known
I'm the idiot

New York City
Been so good for me
I've walked Manhattan
and Manhattan has walked me
She'll treat you so shitty
before revealing her beauty
Anything less
than great success
she's not intrigued

JUST LIKE ME

Too many pillows for sleeping
Push them onto the floor
Too many blankets on my feet
You're always adding one more

    Living with you is a sweet dream
    Fresh cut flowers in the sun
    I've never known so much comfort
    I've always had next to none

You have a closet for linens
Washcloths and robes on the door
How many perfumes and lotions
You're always discovering more

    Living with you is a sweet dream
    Sunday champagne vegan brunch
    I've never known so much smiling
    I've always done next to none

        All your shoes are Italian
        You wear only gold jewelry
        Lately, I get the feeling
        all your men are just like me

You've got a heart for adventure
Fly first class to a distant shore
A hired black car from the airport
New outfit for the guided tour

    Living with you is a sweet dream
    Walking your dog while you're gone
    I've never felt so damn lonely
    I've always been so alone

I know your dreams and your secrets
You are so much to adore
You like to make an appearance
I like to open the door

      Living with you is a sweet dream
      I wonder what is to come
      I've never felt so unneeded
      I've always needed no one

            All your shoes are Italian
            You wear only gold jewelry
            Lately, I get the feeling
            all your men are just like me

MADE FOR TROUBLE

When the road is twistin'
I've got a flowin'
disposition
Carving a hillside
tracing the seaside
I'm smilin'

I get uptight
when everything is alright
Gets on my nerves
On the straightaways
I've got to fight
the urge to swerve

> Maybe I was made for trouble
> Baby, I feel on the edge
> Maybe I'm in love with almost falling
> Baby, I fell for you instead

Nothing but problems
Born to solve them
on the fly
Crashed and burned
so many times
I thought I'd die

Yet I'm still here
I ain't dead yet
Just getting gray
Learning how to survive
with the love of my life
on this straightaway

      Maybe I was made for trouble
      Baby, I feel on the edge
      Maybe I'm in love with almost falling
      Baby, I keep falling for you instead

H O M E

A lamp and a chair
and a table to share
A rug for the floor
and a mirror near the door
We live comfortably
within our means
And it's clean

A small shelf of books
and a kitchen to cook
My boots in the hall
and your guitar on the wall
We are open and free
We have lots of air
to breathe

You eat simple foods
for complex tastes
The white walls are bare
so I can stare out to space
We are living the dream
every moment
We are home

       Maybe you'll settle
       or maybe you'll roam
       Either way it's okay
       your heart is your home
       Keep it uncluttered
       and not filled with junk
       Fill it with space
       for the things that you truly love

There are very few things
so important to me...
The love in your eyes
when you are talking to me
Kiss you once when you come
Kiss you again
when you leave

Albatross

Recalling the idea
of who I used to be
Longing for the dreams
I once clung to so desperately

I never became
half of what I meant to be
But sometimes it seems
like twice as much as I am today

I turned my back
on what set me free
Just been a circle
without a twist of infinity

I cannot deny
my urge to fly
I'm an albatross
trailing a ship on the tides

I took on so much
responsibility
I took the mess that was
my life and made it orderly

This old age feeling
is merely stiffness
from holding the line
and taking care of business

A foot in each world
with a yearning to fly free
The practical man still can
afford a few of his dreams

    I turned my back
    on what set me free
    Just been a circle
    without a twist of infinity

        I cannot deny
        my urge to fly
        I'm an albatross
        A dream not ready to die

Over

Beginnings born in pain
Learning how to live again
Hardly remember

Beaten black and blue
My heart still yearns for you
I'm fucking broken

And the sooner that I die
the sooner new life will arise
My life is over

Though I still find that I resent
being shoved into the present
transformation

Someday it will be okay
Work out fine just like you say
No matter what happens

Because life is always great
It's just our attempt to steer fate
that breaks our hearts

Retrospective

Behind me now
so much awe and wonder
I'm not sure how
I survived the lightning and the thunder
Knowing life
it's heavy
Tears are whelming in my eyes

Behind me now
my mother and my father
My only vows
are to myself and to my daughter
Living life
it's so long
Tears are whelming in my eyes

Behind me now
everything I have adored
I make my bows
to honor all who've gone before
Leaving life
it's too soon
Tears are whelming in my eyes

DARK COCOON

My dark cocoon
Sweat lodge with puke
The steamy place
where I grew wings

Contorted where
I failed to light
a single ember
against the night

Squirm in grease
skin coveralls
Tangled twisted
Trapped in musk

Eternity where
at last dissolves
the membrane
holding back the stars

How in love
with everything
Fluttering
I stretch my wings

I never want
to sleep again
I never want
to sleep again

N O T   L O N E L Y   A N Y M O R E

Tinge of death always in season
I don't need no rhyme, no reason
I know the stranger knocking at the door

Come tomorrow, I'll be gone
Nothing left nothing wrong
And not lonely
anymore

Times you wish that you could hold her
Catch a glimpse over your shoulder
The stranger freezes you right to the core

Sometimes the shadows stay too long
Out of breath, out of songs
Won't be lonely
anymore

There's by far no better thing
to play with Death than hide and seek
He forever hunts you, it is his sport

Sometimes when you're feeling blue
seeking death he hides from you
'til you're not lonely
anymore

BACK TO YOUR ROOTS

Back to your roots
Back to drinking blood
Back to dirty boots
Back to playing rough

Back to long hair
Back to diving deep
Nobody in the driver's seat

   Cribnotes from the underground
   Rolling dice all over town
   Do what you dare not choose
   Do whatever you can't lose

Back to your roots
Back to not needing love
Back to digging a hole
Back to rising above

Back to back women
want you to meet their friend
Nowhere do the good times end

   Living diary of a fiend
   Not a care for what life means
   Do what you dare not choose
   Do whatever you can't lose

Back to black jeans
Back to neon lights
Back to simple things
Back to living at night

Tasting the sugar
on the lips of death
then telling her she's got bad breath

Sidestepping on the razor's edge
Restraint is for those in bondage
Do what you dare not choose
It will all be over soon

B O U R B O N & B I T T E R S

Tonight I'm drinking bourbon and bitters
Occasional shots of jack
Dip down from the clouds
every once in a while
in case I forget where I'm at

I got a gift of gab still unopened
There's plenty of time for that
It's awfully nice
slowly spinning my ice
I'm wide awake taking a nap

      Way up here, nowhere near
      I can see forever
      Forever without you, dear

      Way up here, it's clear
      I should forget her
      But a little bitter
           makes the bourbon
              taste better

The world is slipping off of my shoulders
Hope I'm as light as I feel
It makes my heart sing
to drop everything
Roll on without me crooked wheel

So open up sky I've come to join you
Coming in head over heels
I'm without a care
Disappeared in thin air
Adios Earth it's been too real

Way up here, nowhere near
I can see forever
Forever without you, dear

Way up here, it's clear
I should forget her
But a little bitter
makes the bourbon
taste better

B R O K E N   H E A R T

Everybody has a broken heart
Everybody except you know who
You ain't so tough
if you've not had it rough
Everybody needs a heartbreak or two

Do you see I have a broken heart?
I know the damage feelings can do
I know what love takes
cuz I've made some mistakes
I hope you've made some mistakes too

> Show me the heart that hasn't been broken
> I'll show you a child or a coward
> Show me a heart broken wide open
> and I'll show you the chalice

Go out and get yourself a broken heart
Go out and find someone better than you
You're not alive
until you're broken inside
A heart ain't open til it's broken in two

Everybody needs a broken heart
A muscle grows when you tear it apart
Cowards choose steel
It takes courage to feel
Don't be afraid of a broken heart

> Show me the heart that hasn't been broken
> I'll show you a child or a coward
> Show me a heart broken wide open
> and I'll show you the chalice

DON'T LOOK BACK

Did I look back
to see if you were following
when we were only steps
from being free?

I could nearly hear
our children playing in the woods
The smell of oil paints
lingering

> Don't look back
> There's nothing there
> Don't look back
> There's nothing there
> Perhaps there never was
> Perhaps there...
> Never was

In an instant
I did not know what was happening
All my hopes and dreams
just disappeared

Did I look back
to see if you were following?
Was it all my fault
as I have feared?

> Don't look back
> There's nothing there
> Don't look back
> There's nothing there
> Perhaps there never was
> Perhaps there...
> Never was

MISS JANUARY

It is a Friday
afternoon in January
And soon we won't be married
anymore

I am day-drinking
and I know should not be mixing
Give no fucks and overthinking
It's a bore

> Miss January
> The sun is almost white
> Snow is on the ground
> and it's alright

> Miss January
> So little life in the light
> Soon you will be gone
> it will be night

And when I wake up
one bright morning post the breakup
Like to say just what this fuck up
was ever for

But it's still Friday
afternoon in January
and I know the dark and cold is
coming on

Miss January
The sun is almost white
Snow is on the ground
and I'm alright

Miss January
Enjoy your life in the light
Soon you will be gone
it will be night

FLY HOME

The hallways full of chicken blood
The bedrooms full of bones
In all the years I've known her
she's only let one bird fly home

Now I'm on my way
across infinity
Whenever we cross paths
she always winks at me

> Fly home, fly home
> This world is not for you
> It's for the hungry ones like me

The cavern is a nest of snakes
The darkness wet with steam
Where every hissing breath projects
dreams hanging within reach

Lucky I don't believe
in dreams come true
But a viper pit awaits
to feed off those who do

> Fly home, fly home
> This world is not for you
> It's for the hungry ones like me

All the blood crazed sycophants
trading spittle on the train
Keep exchanging fluids
until they're all the same

I guess I'll never
be a real success
I've got my own reality
exchanging winks with death

> Fly home, fly home
> This world is not for you
> It's for the hungry ones like me

17 (For Khora)

Trouble in the woods
Trouble in town
Don't know why I carry
these troubles around

Just want someone to squeeze
these troubles out of me
Know my heart
Set me free

Everything's too real
when you're seventeen
All of my life is still a dream
And nothing's happening
Nothing's happening

This is my first time
for most anything
All I have are these heavy wings
and barely a breeze
Barely a breeze

I see too much, I feel too deep
I'm up all night can barely sleep
And when I sleep, don't want to wake
In my dreams I don't make mistakes

Trouble in the woods
Trouble in town
Don't know why I carry
these troubles around

Just want someone to squeeze
these troubles out of me
Know my heart
Set me free

Why's time move so slow
when you're seventeen
Every month's an eternity
of waiting to be
Waiting to be

I felt like a child
only yesterday
Do I miss my innocence?
Well, I gave it away
I gave it away

I see too much, I feel too deep
I'm up all night can barely sleep
And when I sleep, don't want to wake
In my dreams I don't make mistakes

Trouble in the woods
Trouble in town
Don't know why I carry
these troubles around

Just want someone to squeeze
these troubles out of me
Know my heart
Set me free

SOUTH OF MOAB

South of Moab
Milky way
Canyon sagebrush
Coyote caves

I'm having the old dreams again
Stretched out on the veranda
with one of my best friends

South of Moab
Feeling bad
Moments silence
for all we had

Don't know if I'll come this way again
Before I'm just another ghost
haunting this ancient land

South of Moab
Milky way
Sometimes darkness
leads the way

BLESS THIS WOUND

Bless this wound
I miss so much
I prefer the pain
to the scar

When I bleed
I feel alive
Otherwise I don't
feel at all

Getting old
I must admit
Ain't got much more time
for this shit

Here's my heart
Do what you will
If you must cut me
aim to kill

Bless this wound
I miss so much
I prefer the pain
to the scar

UNTITILLATED

Fishhooks scratch
Try to snag my skin
The eyes of a billion
fisherman
Lick of lips
Gnash of teeth
I dive down
to the subway reef

No escape
from the prying horde
that tempt and tease
and crave my soul
Look how cute
my shiny skin
Drink my blood
laced with poison

My emptiness
My best defense
My smiling detached
contentment
I reject you
as a bore
Good for nothing
whore for more

Dawn is red
The coming storm
Burn the boats
to keep us warm
Endless walls
So many cells
Playing out
our private hells

My emptiness
My best defense
My smiling detached
contentment
I can see you
through the walls
Drowning in your
shopping malls

I retreat
into real dreams
Weigh the options
strategically
I mutate
I chain react
I wide awake
I don't come back

DELIGHTED

Delighted to be alone
     with all the world
The dirt beneath my feet
     and a crown of clouds
I wasn't here to see yesterday
Cannot wait until tomorrow
     I'll be gone

He who tames the beast in blood
     becomes a god
Dangled from the life tree
     ever upside down
One eye opens, the universe appears
Two eyes open to explore
     like a child

     I'm slashing all these heartstrings
          convinced they tie me down
     I'm worshiping the dark things
          taking me underground
     I'm visiting all my lost friends
          All that's dead and gone
     Burning all my bridges
          since we fly in the beyond

When at last I have returned
     roll away the stone
Want to see the midnight sun
     covered in steam
Not sure I am long for this world
All this flesh and blood
     like a pile of chains

Will the gate remain open
     with all that that entails
I cannot close my eyes
     since my dreams become real
I'm the eyeball in the maelstrom
     Appalled with all the lies
I don't care if we start over
     because we never die

Delighted to be alone
     with all the world
The dirt beneath my feet
     and a crown of clouds
I wasn't here to see yesterday
Cannot wait until tomorrow
     I'll be gone

No Monsters

I might be old
Falling apart
Nothing left but
the path with heart

I let it go
All of the things
that I once thought
were my needs

> I'm opening
> all the doors
> There are no monsters
> anymore

There is a star
and what I do
I'm on my way
I'm passing through

I'm not a place
I'm no one's home
I'm a corridor
to the vast unknown

> I'm opening
> all the doors
> There are no monsters
> anymore

I never knew
I didn't know
The less I am
the more life flows

Until the day
that I dissolve
and see the world
like a newborn child

      I'm opening
      all the doors
      There are no monsters
      anymore

BLONDIE

She's leaving
Taking her bright eyes
and all she's seeing
Heading south tomorrow

Our short meeting
exists in a vacuum
devoid of meaning
if I never see her again

I'm sleeping
Every day's a dream
Nothing repeating
One thing melts into another

    Picking up red raspberries
    Her fingers wrapped in rings
    Each berry so perfectly
    placed between her teeth
    A smile that reminds me
    return to the beach
    Heading south tomorrow

Devoid of meaning
It's all in my head
that's all I'm seeing
Since my big head is empty

Hey blondie
you are so young
So truly friendly
Thank you for the long moment

She's leaving
Taking her bright eyes
and all she's seeing
Heading south tomorrow

Summer Days

I was surprised
by the passing of time
It unraveled so fast
Summer days beneath
      the breezy leaves
Asleep in the grass

A bite to eat
and we're hitting the streets
spending all of our cash
Summer nights beneath
      the dusty stars
Just lookin' to crash

      Would it be different if we were different?
      I think we're pretty much the same
      We all have our moments
      We all have our graves

This is our life
following our delight
There is not much to grasp
We cannot take the
      seasons with us
We just leave our past

I was surprised
by the passing of time
It unraveled so fast

Ashes

When you rise from the ashes
what you were is blown away
For a moment you are starlight
in the middle of the day

No longer bound
No longer fragile
An empty vessel
Crystal clear

For a moment
feel like forever
Until that moment
disappears

When you are weary of rebuilding
endless somebodies to be
That only beckon to the lightning
Becoming things not meant to be

Follow the moon
across the tidepools
Beyond the narrows
of these dreams

Lose yourself
in morning sunlight
Endless
possibilities